INSIGHT GUIDES

Instant
ROME

APA PUBLICATIONS

Part of the Langenscheidt Publishing Group

L

07471-891821

Via De la Vizi
near Spanish Steps.

AS Roma Store
Appo Nuova
Piazza Colonna

CONTENTS

Compiled by Clare Peel
Photography by Bill Wassman
Additional photography by
    Frances Gransden
Cover photograph:
    Robert Harding Picture Library

As every effort is made to provide accu-
rate information in this publication, we
would appreciate it if readers would call
our attention to any errors that may occur
by communicating with Apa Publications,
PO Box 7910, London SE1 1WE,
England. Fax: (44) 20 7403 0290;
e-mail: insight@apaguide.demon.co.uk

Distributed in the UK & Ireland by
GeoCenter International Ltd
The Viables Centre, Harrow Way
Basingstoke, Hampshire RG22 4BJ
Fax: (44 1256) 817-988

Distributed in the United States by
Langenscheidt Publishers, Inc.
46–35 54th Road
Maspeth, NY 11378
Tel: (718) 784-0055. Fax: (718) 784-0640

Worldwide distribution enquiries:
APA Publications GmbH & Co. Verlag KG
Singapore Branch, Singapore
38 Joo Koon Road, Singapore 628990
Tel: (65) 865-1600. Fax: (65) 861-6438

Printed in Singapore by
Insight Print Services (Pte) Ltd
38 Joo Koon Road, Singapore 628990
Tel: (65) 865-1600. Fax: (65) 861-6438

www.insightguides.com

THE ETERNAL CITY

Dubbed the Eternal City by poets and artists, Rome is one of the most exhilarating and romantic travel destinations in the world. With its soft, ochre-coloured *palazzi*, classical colonnades and dramatic centrepieces such as the Colosseum and the Pantheon, it is a city that inspires the mind, appeals to the senses and captures the heart. As is frequently pointed out on souvenirs and T-shirts, Roma is *amor* spelt backwards.

An Attractive Heritage

Home to the Vatican and once hub of a great empire, Rome has been at the centre of European civilisation for well over 2,000 years. It has attracted travellers for a millennium. Pilgrims came during the Middle Ages – in the "Holy Year" of 1300 alone, some 2 million pilgrims visited the city – and by the 17th century it was seen as a finishing school for European courtiers and gentlemen, the source "of policy, learning, music, architecture and limning [painting], with other perfections which she dispertheth to the rest of Europe".

During the 19th century Rome attracted a stream of poets, writers, painters and sculptors of all nationalities, including the German poet, novelist and dramatist J.W. von Goethe, the French author Stendhal and the US-born British novelist Henry James. However, the English Romantics – notably Byron, Keats and Shelley –

Left: *the legendary Julius Caesar*

were especially drawn to the city, relishing the pathetic charm of greatness brought to its knees. Rome offered them a retreat from the repressive morality of England, and they saw in Rome's ruins a reflection of themselves: Romantic exiles misunderstood and despised by their own country.

Capital of the Eternal Seductress

In Italy itself, Rome is something of a loner, both indulged and resented by the rest of the country. The city is neither northern nor southern, and, although it is Italy's capital, it is not considered as sophisticated as fast-paced Milan, the centre of Italian fashion and design.

Rome has all the problems of a major metropolis and a few more besides. It has a fabulous archaeological and architectural legacy to maintain, which is both a burden and a source of pride. While traffic pollution erodes the monuments – turning marble into limestone – the civil authorities fight to protect them.

Above: the Fori Imperiali

As the British journalist George Armstrong remarked: "Rome is the only European capital which each year must spend millions of pounds restoring ruins – restoring them at least to their state of ruin of 100 years ago."

As a result of the Jubilee (or Holy) Year 2000, however, Rome is now resplendent. The 2000th anniversary of the birth of Jesus Christ was celebrated in unique style with the refurbishment of more than 700 temples, churches, galleries and archaeological sites, fittingly paving the capital's way for the next 2,000 years.

Roman Holiday

Rome is crammed with great sights and in no other city are the accumulated layers of history so evident. Every corner and crest seems to lead to a world-famous monument, church or square. However, for first-time visitors trying to grapple with the layout of the city's 12 hills – not the seven usually attributed to it – Rome can seem confusing. The best way to orientate oneself is to look upon Via del Corso as a spine, with the leafy Villa Borghese quarter at the top, the archaeological zone at the bottom, the Centro Storico to the west, Piazza di Spagna to the east, and the Vatican and Trastevere on the far bank of the River Tiber. There's so much to see that it's advisable to spend at least a week here to do the city justice.

Right: *fronting the Vittoriano monument*

HISTORICAL HIGHLIGHTS

31BC–AD14 Augustus founds the Empire. The arts flourish, and roads are constructed across the realm.

AD64 After setting fire to Rome, Nero builds his Domus Aurea, the "Golden House".

69–79 Vespasian builds the Flavian Amphitheatre (the Colosseum). The Arch of Titus  is erected in the Forum to commemorate the destruction of Jerusalem in AD 70 by Vespasian and his son, Titus.

98–117 The Roman Empire achieves its greatest territorial expansion under the Emperor Trajan. It extends as far north as the East Friesian islands, east to Mesopotamia, south to North Africa and west to Spain and Britain. The arts flourish.

117–38 Hadrian builds walls to secure the Empire's borders.

161–80 Marcus Aurelius.

193–211 Septimius Severus.

250 Persecution of the Christians under Emperor Decius.

284–305 Diocletian's reign. The empire begins its decline and the tetrarchy is introduced.

312 Constantine (280–337) defeats Maxentius. Christianity is officially recognised. In 330 Byzantium, now Constantinople, becomes the Roman Empire's capital.

395 The Empire is split. In 404, Ravenna is made the capital of the Western part.

410 Rome is taken by invading Visigoths under King Alaric.

455 The city is plundered by the Vandals.

476 Fall of the Western Roman

Above: temple to Venus, Foro di Cesare

Empire. Power is assumed by the Germans.

536 Rome is captured by Byzantium. East Roman rule is re-established in Italy.

590–604 Pope Gregory the Great protects Rome by making peace with the Lombards.

750s Pepin the Short, king of the Franks, returns to the church the lands taken away from it by the Lombards. He then lays the foundation of the temporal sovereignty of the popes (Papal States) by giving the pope the exarchate of Ravenna.

800 Charlemagne is crowned emperor. The Roman Empire is restored in name.

1309 Clement V removes the seat of the papacy to Avignon in the south of France. The so-called "second Babylonian captivity" of the popes begins.

1377 Gregory XI returns to Rome.

15th century Rome undergoes a new phase of prosperity during the Renaissance. The Popes attract artists including Bellini, Botticelli, Da Vinci, Michelangelo, Palladio, Raphael and Titian to

Above: ruins in the gardens of Palazzo Farnese, Palatine Hill

Rome to decorate the city.

1527 Charles V's army sacks Rome (Sacco di Roma).

1585–90 There is a brief period of prosperity under Pope Sixtus, swiftly followed by a decline in the city's political, cultural and economic importance. The Italian peninsula splits into smaller states. Rome is made capital of the Papal States.

1798–9 Rome becomes a French-style republic.

1801 Pope Pius VII concludes a concordat with Napoleon to preserve the independence of Rome and the Papal States. Under Napoleon's son Rome is made part of the French Empire.

1814 The Papal States are restored to Pope Pius VII at the Congress of Vienna.

1870–1 Rome and the Papal States are conquered. Rome becomes the capital of the new kingdom of Italy. The popes live as prisoners in the Vatican.

1922 Fascist leader Benito Mussolini assumes power.

1929 The Vatican is made an independent sovereign state.

1939–45 World War II. In 1943 Mussolini is placed under arrest and the Allies land in southern Italy. The Allies liberate Rome on 4 June 1944.

1945 Mussolini is hanged.

1946 After a referendum, Italy becomes a republic, with Rome as the capital; King Umberto II is exiled to Portugal.

1978 Aldo Moro, Italy's prime minister and head of the Christian Democrat Party, is kidnapped by terrorists and killed. Cardinal Karol Wojtyla becomes the first Polish pope (John Paul II).

1981 An assassination attempt is made on the pontiff in St Peter's Square.

Above: Madonna del Parto, Sant' Agostino

1994 Media magnate Silvio Berlusconi is elected premier. By late 1994 he is forced to resign and in 1997 he receives a suspended prison sentence for fraud.

1995 Giulio Andreotti, Roman power-broker and seven-times Italian premier, goes on trial for Mafia association.

1996 The first left-wing government in Italian post-war history is elected.

1998 The centre-left coalition that led Italy through the economic resurgence of the late 1990s and to the first tier of fiscal stability in Europe gives way. The former communist leader Massimo D'Alema is named prime minister.

2000 Millions flock to Rome to take part in the Holy Year celebrations.

2001 The media mogul Silvio Berlusconi, Italy's wealthiest citizen, is re-elected *(see entry for 1994)* as prime minister, heading the centre-right House of Liberties alliance.

Above: *fresco by Pinturicchio, Santa Maria in Aracoeli*

PEOPLE AND CULTURE

The Archetypal Roman

In the popular imagination, Ancient Rome was peopled by emperors and orators, poets and politicians, patricians and plebeians, valiant gladiators and avaricious tax collectors. Today, outsiders see Romans as typically phlegmatic and philosophical, shrewd and sly, suave and duplicitous, jaded and decadent, vulgar yet vibrant. Some of these contemporary traits are believed to be deep rooted: Emperor Vespasian personified Roman shrewdness by charging citizens for using public latrines.

Modern-day Romans claim that the "real" Romans are consigned to the history books. In the 19th century Rome had the smallest middle class of any major European city. However, by 1900 a population boom meant that the number of inhabitants had doubled, swollen by the exodus from the south after World War II.

Above: *taking it easy, near Piazza Santa Maria in Trastevere*

In the 1960s, the population reached 2 million and by the 1990s it had topped 3 million. As a consequence, Romans with long family histories in the city are scarce and they are treasured for their authenticity. Most modern Romans are of mixed ancestry, with roots going back fewer than just five generations.

Whether spoilt, opinionated, resilient and with only the weakest links to the Romans of yesteryear or not, the inhabitants of the Italian capital certainly know how to live. They have made Rome, in essence a city of illusion and disillusion, into one of the most culturally rich, architecturally impressive and vibrant of European capitals.

The Daily Routine

The day in Rome typically begins and ends in traffic jams because the city centre, *Roma intra muros*, based on the "Seven Hills", is periodically closed to cars. To avoid the traffic chaos, many Romans resort to *motorini* (mopeds). En route, the popular image shows them fortified by fiercely strong coffee and several *cornetti* (sweet croissants) in a bar.

The average Roman has an inbuilt resistance to Milanese efficiency, schedules and short lunch breaks. The Roman working day has to accommodate a leisurely lunch: after an urgent telephone command to *butta la pasta!* (put on the pasta) your typical Roman rushes home to ensure that the pasta is suitably *al dente*. Between 1pm and 2pm, the ensuing gridlock tangles the telephone lines and traffic but leaves the streets deserted

Right: the traditional greeting

between 2pm and 3pm. Local lore has it that the *siesta* was championed by the Vatican to ensure that after a snooze in his mistress's arms, the dutiful husband would return to his wife in the evening, thus preserving the sanctity of family life. Whatever the reason, once refreshed by a *siesta*, Romans often work from 4 until 8pm.

A City of Religious Sceptics

As a sovereign state and the capital of Catholicism, the Vatican celebrates its triumph over paganism. However, these sentiments are not shared by typically sceptical Romans. In keeping with their eclectic past, Romans tend to be ritualistic rather than religious, formalistic rather than faithful.

Today, the Vatican is seen as a political institution, the corporate arm of the papacy. Anti-clerical attitudes have been confirmed by the Vatican financial and political scandals of the early 1980s and by the conservatism of Pope John Paul II.

Above: the grandeur of the Vatican

The city may have more than 900 churches, but only 3 percent of Romans regularly attend Mass. If the papacy intrudes on daily Roman life, it is only as a source of sexual proscription or a cause of traffic congestion. To the world-weary Romans, the Wednesday papal audience simply serves to clog the city streets with yet more traffic.

When Pope John Paul II was almost assassinated in 1981, the news barely impinged on the city's preparations for a major football match. The typical response from Roma fans was: *"Il papa è morto? Se ne fa un altro."* (The Pope is dead? Well, they'll just have to find another one.) The Vatican State across the Tiber from central Rome is held in low esteem. As local Roman wisdom has it: "Faith is made here but believed elsewhere."

Political Parasites

Some view Roman politics with an equally cynical eye. According to the Roman novelist Alberto Moravia, "Rome is an administrative city dominated by two institutions: the State and the Church."

As a temporal and spiritual capital, the city seems a harmonious spot. Yet as the political capital, Rome enjoys a reputation as the flea on the back of long-suffering northern Italy. The prejudice is fed by tales of a bloated bureaucracy. In Italian eyes, the Romans are greedy parasites and power-brokers bent on keeping the administrative spoils within the family. The city is smothered by a web of

Right: *making a statement*

political mismanagement and the culture of corruption, embracing the stranglehold of clientalistic contracts and the misappropriation of public funds.

Stolen Culture

Ironically, although the Romans have always been artistic connoisseurs, they have also long been cultural raiders who see no need to stoop to creativity themselves. Real Roman artists are rare, restricted to Pietro Cavallini, the medieval artist who created the mosaics in Santa Maria in Trastevere, or Giulio Sartorio, whose modern frescoes adorn the parliamentary chamber at Palazzo di Montecitorio.

In classical times, Greek art, philosophy and poetry shaped Roman culture while naturalistic Etruscan statuary inspired Roman busts. During the Renaissance, papal patrons lured the

greatest painters and sculptors from Florence, Milan or Urbino to Rome. Pope Julius II transformed St Peter's with the help of Tuscans such as Michelangelo.

According to the novelist Alberto Moravia, "Rome receives everything yet gives nothing back." This talent for theft, also known as cultural assimilation, can be traced to Ancient Roman practices and a propensity for hedging bets with all manner of alien gods. In particular, the *exoratio* was a favoured imperial battle ritual in which the enemy's gods were invoked and invited over to the Roman camp. In

Above: *statues in the Musei Capitoline, Piazza del Campidoglio*

return for victory, the Romans transported their vanquished foe's idols to a dusty yet cosmopolitan collection on the Capitoline Hill. There, they were worshipped as assimilated Roman gods.

La Cucina Romana

Most Romans are omnivorous but, according to food critic Leo Pescarolo, they have "neither the culture nor the patience to invent a refined cuisine". They are certainly not culinary snobs, and a typical motto is: "The more you spend, the worse you eat."

Although most hotels offer continental breakfast, Italians have no tradition of breakfast food. An espresso and a croissant (*un caffè e un cornetto*) take most people through to midday. Lunch is usually served from 12–2.30pm, dinner from 8–10.30pm, and though menus are organised into *antipasti* (appetisers), *primi* (pastas and soups), *secondi* (meat and fish dishes), *contorni* (vegetables) and *dolci* (desserts), you should never feel obliged to select a dish from each category. Few Italians eat full sit-down meals more than once a day.

Above: *ice-cream culture*

Service is included in the bill unless otherwise noted on the menu. It is customary to leave a small amount of change as a tip, but nothing like the 10–15 percent common in other countries.

The old cover charge, called *pane e coperto*, has been abolished, but it still appears on many menus. Keep an eye out, though, as in many cases it has turned into a charge for bread. (If you wish, you may refuse both the bread and the fee; otherwise consider it a part of eating out.)

TYPICAL DISHES

A considerable portion of the local cuisine involves offal. While dishes including *rigatoni con pajata* (pasta with veal intestines) and *trippa alla romana* (tripe with tomato sauce, Roman mint and pecorino) are long-time local favourites, you will find that most restaurants in the centre of town tend to avoid such specialities in favour of dishes from other parts of the country that are more familiar to their clientele, such as pasta with pesto sauce, risotto and polenta.

Pricey restaurants offer adventurous dishes with long names, but the menu of a typical Roman eatery tells a different, less complicated story: *spaghetti alla carbonara* (with bacon, egg and pecorino cheese), *bucatini alla gricia* (with *guanciale* – cured pork jowl), *cacio e pepe* (with pecorino cheese and black pepper) and *all'amatriciana* (with *guanciale* or bacon and tomato sauce) all share an undeniable simplicity.

Also popular are *spaghetti alle vongole* (clams tossed with

Above: a tricky dish to handle

spaghetti and olive oil), *pesce azzurro* (fish) baked in the oven (*al forno)* or cooked on the grill (*ai ferri* or *alla griglia*), *saltimbocca alla romana* (veal with prosciutto and sage) and *coda alla vaccinara* (braised oxtail in tomato and celery sauce). The meat to try is *abbacchio* (milk-fed lamb), roasted with herbs and garlic, or *alla scottadito* (grilled chops). *Gnocchi alla romana* (potato dumplings in a meat sauce) are traditionally prepared on Thursdays, while it's customary to serve *baccalà* (salt cod) on Fridays.

Save room for your greens, however, which abound in Rome's produce markets all year long and find their way to the table in basic preparations, often steamed or blanched, then briefly sauteed. The Romans are the undisputed masters of the artichoke (*carciofo*), in season from November to April and traditionally prepared in several ways, among them *carciofi alla giudia* (deep fried) and *carciofi alla romana* (stuffed with garlic and Roman mint and then stewed).

Above: *delights of the Roman delicatessen*

Though the Neapolitans are credited with inventing pizza, the Romans still eat their fair share. There are more *pizzerie* than restaurants in the city, and there is even a specific pizza from the capital – plate-sized, rolled very thin and flat and baked in a wood-burning stove (*forno a legna*). A Neapolitan pizza is thicker and softer, with a raised border. A night out at a *pizzeria* (few are open for lunch) is a quintessential Roman experience.

Appetisers and desserts get little attention in most Roman restaurants. A few common starters are melon or figs with *prosciutto* and *fiori di zucca* (deep-fried courgette flowers filled with mozzarella and anchovies). Popular desserts are *torta di ricotta* (ricotta tart), *panna cotta* (eggless firm custard made of cream and served with a fruit sauce) and the more-familiar *tiramisu* (Italian espresso trifle).

Gelato (ice-cream) is viewed not so much as a dessert as an afternoon or after-dinner snack to accompany a stroll around town. Accordingly, *gelaterie* are never far away and stay open until late.

Drinking Holes

There seems to be a wine bar on almost every corner in Rome. Bars not only serve wine and hot drinks, they also offer a great alternative to a restaurant meal. You can usually

Above: *ready for first orders*

choose from about a dozen wines available by the glass (or from more than a thousand different labels by the bottle) and a wonderful selection of high-quality cheeses, cured meats, and smoked fish, as well as soups, salads, quiches,

gratins and home-made desserts. The local Roman wines, of which those from Frascati are the most famous, are often lamented in guidebooks as not being as good as they once were. On the contrary, they are probably better than they have ever been, but pale in comparison with wines produced in other parts of the country.

Note that you will pay more in a bar or cafe if you choose to sit down than if you remain standing at the bar. Drinking on the terrace usually incurs a further premium.

Nightlife

Roman nightlife tends to be fun rather than frenzied, laid-back rather than sophisticated. Apart from a few privileged or exclusive clubs, the nightclub scene is far less elegant than in Paris, less assured than in Munich, and far less adventurous than in Berlin, London or New York. As a general rule, nightclubs attract a wealthy, sophisticated, middle-class clientele, whereas discos are predominantly for the young. Yet within this distinction there is considerable variety.

Above: laid-back Roman nightlife

Geographically, it is difficult to label areas as nightlife quarters. The big exception to this is Trastevere, which has long been the destination for Romans in search of a good time. However, Testaccio is fast taking its place as a slightly more "alternative" location. The historic quarters around Piazza Navona, the Pantheon and Piazza di Spagna (the Spanish Steps) also contain a number of popular bars and clubs.

The Via Veneto, celebrated in Fellini's movie *La Dolce Vita*, is now somewhat staid. However, the quarter is still home to certain elegant nightclubs and piano bars, which tend to be more popular with American visitors than with Romans.

Roman nightlife can be so low-key that residents are happy to wander through the beautiful historic centre, pausing to chat, greet friends, glance in shop windows, eat the occasional ice-cream and nonchalantly stop for a drink, a *digestivo* or even just a restorative *tisane* (herbal or fruit tea).

Sport: A National Obsession

Sport, particularly football, plays a important part in the lives of the Italian people as a whole. When there's a football match in progress, don't be surprised to see Romans of all ages with

Above: regulation cigarette and shades at Porta Portese

radios pressed against their ears, eager to hear the latest result. In the event of one of Rome's two home teams – Roma or Lazio – winning, then the peace of the afternoon is likely to be broken by honking car horns and a great deal of shouting.

Aside from football, Rome hosts a major event on both the men's and women's international tennis circuits. Both events are known as the Italian Open and they take place at the Foro Italico during May. You will never see another tennis event quite like it – unlike Wimbledon, it's not a case of a polite clap here and there, the crowd applaud and jeer to their heart's content.

The Fashion Scene

Italy's fashion industry is revered the world over, and while most business in centred on Milan, there are a handful of top designers who have made their base in Rome. The most famous of these is probably Valentino, who opened his Roman studio in 1959 and has enjoyed success ever since. His high-profile clients have

included the actresses Sophia Loren and Audrey Hepburn and America's former first lady Jackie Kennedy.

Other top Rome-based names to look for include Sorelle Fontana, Fendi and Laura Biagiotti. All the other well-known Italian designers, among them Versace, Armani and Trussardi, also have boutiques in Rome, mostly around Via Condotti.

Right: *that infamous Roman chic*

Shopping

Rome may not be such a renowned shopping mecca as Milan or Florence, nor so famed for the production of any particular artisanal goods, but most of the major designers have boutiques in the capital *(see page 21)*, and prices are thought to be more competitive than in northern towns. Particularly attractive buys include books on art and architecture, stylish kitchenware, marbled notepaper from a *cartoleria*, a stylish modern lamp, or an old print. Regional wines, cheeses and olive oil are also good

value. Other good-value buys include leatherware, designer luggage, ceramics, glassware, lighting, inlaid-marble tables, gold jewellery and *objets d'art*. For those with the time and excess baggage allowance to spare, browsing for textiles, antiques and hand-crafted furniture can also be a pleasant way of spending time in the capital.

It is generally not possible to return merchandise for refund or exchange, and service in shops – particularly clothing shops – all too often ranges from barely adequate to truly awful.

Via del Corso, Piazza di Spagna and Via del Babuino mark the boundaries of the

Above: *shopping for stylish leather goods*

classic window-shopping area. Here you can find everything from designer jeans to beautiful hand-crafted jewellery and antique furniture. Nearby Via della Croce and Via del Corso offer fashion at more accessible prices. The streets

around Piazza Navona, the Pantheon and Campo de' Fiori are good for unusual hand-crafted artisanal wares and a range of smaller boutiques. The Campo de' Fiori quarter is still home to craftsmen, art restorers and market traders – a traditional working-class mix that is fast dying out in trendy Trastevere.

Via del Babuino, Via Margutta, Via Giulia, Via dei Coronari and Via del Pellegrino are the main streets for antiques, *objets d'art* and paintings, while Via Nazionale is an undistinguished but relatively inexpensive shopping street, offering a wide range of basic clothing.

Via Cola di Rienzo, the thoroughfare linking the Vatican with the Tiber (and Piazza del Popolo on the other bank) is lined with small boutiques and elegant shops selling a wide range of goods. Along Via della Conciliazione, the street linking the Vatican with Castel Sant'Angelo, a wide range of religious artefacts including Vatican coins, statues, stamps, religious books and souvenirs can be had. Similar objects are on sale on the streets around the Vatican itself and on Via dei Cestari, which runs

Above: *timeless elegance*

between the Pantheon and Largo Argentina. Via del Governo Vecchio is one of the best streets for stylish second-hand clothes, as are the markets at Porta Portese *(see page 48)* and Via Sannio.

Getting Your Bearings

It sometimes seems that all Roman roads lead to Piazza Venezia. This can produce traffic chaos, but from a visitor's point of view the square is a useful orientation point at the centre of ancient, medieval and modern Rome. To the south of Piazza Venezia, the three roads, Via dei Fori Imperiali, Via di San Gregorio and Via delle Terme, thread between the greatest monuments of ancient Rome to the Terme di Caracalla.

Northwards, Via del Corso runs through the commercial heart of modern Rome to Piazza del Popolo. To the west, Corso Vittorio Emanuele II leads through the heart of medieval Rome and across the Tiber (Tevere) both to St Peter's and the Vatican. Eastwards are Via Nazionale, Piazza della Repubblica and Piazza del Cinquecento to Stazione Termini.

An easy – and pleasant – way to get an overview of the capital is to walk up the Gianicolo (Janiculum Hill) behind Trastevere. There are great views of the whole city from the dome of St Peter's via the Pantheon to the Colosseum.

Above: *Piazza del Popolo*

In much of the city centre the best way to get around is on foot. The majority of the main sights are within walking distance of each other, and you can use public transport for longer distances.

Although some parts of the city centre are – in theory – pedestrianised, you're best advised not to rely too heavily on this. A considerable number of moped riders (and even some car drivers) make their way through pedestrian streets regardless, as if they are exempt from the traffic restrictions. You need to cross the road with confidence, staring down nearby drivers: if you wait timidly at a pedestrian crossing for the traffic to stop, you may well spend the whole of the day there.

As the saying goes, "When in Rome, do as the Romans do," and if you behave like a local and manage the roads with confidence, you should get along fine.

Above: *the nippiest way to get around*

A–Z OF ROME

Arco di Costantino (Arch of Constantine)

Set at the northern end of Via di San Gregorio, near the Colosseum, is the Arco di Costantino. Although the arch was erected in 312, after Constantine's victory over Maxentius at the Ponte Milvio, most of the sculptures adorning it come from monuments from the days of Trajan, Hadrian and Marcus Aurelius. This reflects the drop in the level of craftsmanship by Constantine's reign.

Arco di Settimio Severo (Arch of Septimius Severus)

Just off Via di San Gregrorio looms the Arco di Settimio Severo, erected in AD 203 to honour the tenth anniversary of the ascent to the throne of Emperor Septimius Severus (AD 193–211). The arch measures 25 metres (75 ft) wide, 10 metres (30 ft) deep and 20 metres (60 ft) high, and bears reliefs depicting the campaigns of the emperor against the Arabs and the Parthians.

It also features inscriptions celebrating the victories of the emperor and his two sons, Geta and Caracalla. Caracalla later had his brother murdered in the arms of their mother and placed him under *damnatio memoriae* (exile from memory) by ordering all inscriptions to Geta to be deleted from monuments and replaced with laudatory titles to himself. You can still see the chisel marks on the inscriptions, which were originally inlaid with metal.

The Aventine Hill

The most southerly of Rome's hills, the Aventine has become one of the most desirable places to live in Rome, being both con-

Left: the enduringly impressive Colosseum

veniently located close to the city centre and surprisingly peaceful. In the 3rd century BC, the hill was included within the city walls – mainly for strategic reasons – and was virtually uninhabited until the lower classes, in conflict with the nobility, retreated to this area to organise the first general strikes.

During the Republican years, the Aventine Hill was the site of secret meetings and midnight rituals of the Dionysian and Bacchian cults. The wild, drunken orgies came to public attention in 186 BC and thousands of participants were put to death. Imperial Rome constructed magnificent temples on the hill and the aristocracy built their luxury villas here. In many of these palatial buildings, Christians secretly set up their first meetings.

The area continued to prosper until 410, when Alaric and the Goths destroyed the hill, leaving it uninhabited. In the following centuries, several churches were built on sacred sites. It is only in recent years that the Aventine has regained its smart appeal.

Above: *Piazza San Pietro, seen from the roof of the basilica*

Basilica di San Pietro (St Peter's)

See Vaticano, pages 57–9

Cafe de Paris

Located at Via Veneto 90, the Cafe de Paris is the archetypal Roman coffee house. It starred in Federico Fellini's classic film *La Dolce Vita* and has been living on the profits ever since. This area is not really the fashion mecca it once was but if you want to watch life go by on Via Veneto, this is a comfortable place to linger over an expensive coffee.

Campidoglio (Capitol Hill)

A good place to start a tour of Rome's ancient foundations is Campidoglio. At only 50 metres (150 ft) high, this is the smallest hill in Rome, but in ancient times it looked quite different. Cliffs of tufa fell down steeply on all sides of its twin crowns and on the southern crown of the hill stood the Tempio di Giove (Temple of Jupiter), which was the religious hub of the state.

Originally as big as a football pitch, the temple was begun by the Etruscan kings and dedicated in 509 BC, the first year of the Republic. Behind its six-pillared, south-facing front lay a great anteroom that led to the shrines of Jupiter, Juno and Minerva. Here, the ancient Romans honoured the goddess Juno Moneta, who is supposed to have warned them of an attack by Gauls in 390 BC by making her sacred geese honk. The mint also stood here, hence the word *moneta*, meaning money.

Above: *statue in the Piazza del Campidoglio*

Every New Year's Day, the consuls were inaugurated in a formal ceremony on the Capitol. The triumphal processions followed Via Sacra, the holy road, coming up the hill from the Foro Romano (Roman Forum).

Cappella Sistina (Sistine Chapel)

See Vaticano, pages 57–61

Castel Sant' Angelo

The imposing Castel Sant' Angelo, with its magnificent position along the Tiber, is a symbol of Rome. Construction started on the building in AD 123 and, 16 years later, it became Emperor Hadrian's mausoleum. It has since been used as a fortress, a prison and as the Pope's hiding place in times of trouble.

Thanks to patronage from the popes, many of the rooms – such as the Sala Paolina painted by Del Vaga in 1544 – are beautifully frescoed. The castle also now houses a military museum, which is open daily from 8am–10pm.

***Above:** approach to the Castel Sant' Angelo*

Catacombs

Contrary to popular belief, the catacombs were not used for worship, nor as places of refuge during times of Christian persecution, but for simple funeral ceremonies – they were built underground to save space on the surface. The catacombs were built outside the city – usually in the grounds of rich Christians or Christian sympathisers – because the law forbade burials within the city limits.

Among the rows of shelves for the dead, you can see many little "tombs", used for the tragically high number of infant deaths. The largest and most imposing "tombs" were typically reserved for martyrs – these last were mostly reburied in Roman churches during the Middle Ages.

Catacombs open to the public include the Catacombe di San Sebastiano and the Catacombe di Domitilla, both of which are in the Via Appia area. Around 1 mile (1.5 km) southeast of the church of Domine Quo Vadis, between Via Appia and Via Ardenatina, are the Catacombe di San Callisto.

In the Cripta dei Papi (Crypt of the Popes), inscriptions of at least 10 bishops of Rome from the 3rd and 4th centuries have been discovered. Among them is the first documented use of the title "Pope" for the Bishop of Rome (dating from 298). *www.catacombe.roma.it*

Right: *in the Catacombe di San Callisto*

Centro Storico (Historic Centre)

Covering the area within the city walls, the Centro Historico section of Rome has been continuously inhabited since the Middle Ages, when the population of the city numbered a few tens of thousands, right through to modern times. Roughly speaking, it is contained by the great bend of the Tiber west of Via del Corso.

The Centro Storico is home to many fine churches and Renaissance palaces, and its tangle of streets and alleyways has been the home of the craft guilds since the streets or quarters were full of *botteghe* (workshops) of the same trade. This still holds true – though the trades have changed somewhat – around Via dei Coronari and Via dell'Orso, where there are antique shops and fairs, and Piazza della Fontanella Borghese, which has a print market.

One of the most interesting streets from this point of view is Via dei Cestari (connecting the Pantheon and Largo Argentina),

which is lined with shops selling religious raiments and equipment for the Catholic priesthood. Many facades incorporate old guild signs or pieces of ancient marble.

Colosseo (Colosseum)

Originally called the Amphitheatrum Flavium, the Colosseum was the site of gladiatorial combats featuring criminals, prisoners of war, slaves and, sometimes,

Above: the busy Via del Corso

somewhat foolhardy volunteers. The Emperor Vespasian ordered the arena to be built on the site of the artificial lake of Nero's Domus Aurea (Golden House). The elliptical site measures 190 metres (570 ft) long by 150 metres (450 ft) wide. Following Roman architectural taste, Tuscan, Ionic and Corinthian pillars were placed one above the other.

In AD 80, Titus opened the Colosseum with 100 days of games and more than 5,000 animals are supposed to have been slaughtered during that period. The theatre had 80 entrances and could seat between 55,000 and 73,000 spectators.

Today, the walls of the various dungeons, cages and passageways – gruesome reminders of the centuries-long slaughter that took place here – can be seen through the caved-in floor of the arena. The Ludus Magnus, the nearby training ground of the gladiators, complete with a mini amphitheatre, was connected to the arena by a tunnel.

Above: *the monumental Colosseum*

The amphitheatre was filled early in the morning, mostly by men. The lower seats were reserved for senators, civil servants in official dress and the Vestals; other women sat at the top. Shortly before the games began, the emperor and his followers would enter the amphitheatre, and the spectators would show their reverence by clapping, cheering, waving cloths and chanting their sovereign's honorifics.

If one of the gladiators tried to retreat into the underground chamber, he was pushed forward with red-hot irons. Spectacles began with cries of "Hail Caesar, those about to die salute you." The gladiators mostly fought to the death. A wounded gladiator could beg for mercy by lifting a finger of his left hand. If the crowd waved handkerchiefs, he was saved. Thumbs down meant death. Next came the wild beasts, which were made to fight either one another or humans – armed or unarmed.

Gladiatorial combat was banned in AD 438, and the last-recorded animal show took place in 523. The reserved seats in

Above: *gladiatorial dress*

the lower tiers still bear the names of 195 senators from the time of Odoacer (AD 476–483). In later times the amphitheatre became the fortress of the Frangipani family and a quarry for Palazzo Venezia, Palazzo della Cancelleria, the harbour of Ripetta and St Peter's.

The holes in the masonry testify to the shortage of metal in the Middle Ages, when the Colosseum's clamps were knocked out and recycled. In 1744 Benedict XIV consecrated the arena to the memory of Christian martyrs who died there, though modern research has failed to prove widescale sacrifice of Christians.

Fontana di Trevi (Trevi Fountain)

Rome's most celebrated fountain was immortalised in the 1960 film *La Dolce Vita*, when the curvaceous Swedish actress Anita Ekberg plunged into its waters. Thousands of tourists have wanted to make their own big splash in the fountain ever since, but a 1987 order from the Assessor for Tourism requires visitors to respect the "dignity and cleanliness of the city of Rome" – in other words, you should keep the top half of your body covered and your feet out of public fountains. If you do try and put a foot in the water, a whistle blast from the city police, the *Vigili Urbani*, will stop you in your tracks. However, no-one will prevent you from throwing a coin into the fountain, which, according to tradition, is supposed to ensure your return to Rome.

Right: *the Fontana di Trevi*

The water in the fountain comes from the ancient aqueduct built by Agrippa in 19 BC to supply his baths near the Pantheon. According to legend, the water was called Acqua Vergine, after the girl (*virgo* in Latin) who discovered the spring's source. It was not until the 18th century that the fountain was added. Designed by Nicola Salvi, it was completed in 1762 and depicts Salubrity and Abundance, flanked by the huge central figure of Neptune.

Fori Imperiali (Imperial Fora)

The Fori Imperiali are mostly buried under Via dei Fori Imperiali, but there is still much to see from the road.

The first "imperial" forum, the **Foro di Cesare** (Forum of Caesar), was built in 51 BC by Julius Caesar, when the original forum became too small for Rome's growing population.

The new forum was dedicated in 46 BC, despite being unfinished; it was completed under Augustus (23 BC–AD 14). Following Hellenistic models, this forum was square-shaped and enclosed by pillars. On the west side stood the Temple of Venus Genetrix, built because Caesar believed himself to be a descendant of the goddess. Excavations have uncovered only one-quarter of the site

The **Foro di Traiano** (Trajan's Forum), the biggest of the fora – so large, in fact, that a small hill between Quirinal and Campidoglio had to be removed so that it could be built – is located off

Above: the lofty Colonna Traiana

Via Alessandrina, east of Via dei Fori Imperiali. To the northwest, the forum was bound by the Basilica Ulpia, a hall with five naves. In its western apse, the Atrium Libertatis, slaves were emancipated. Many market stalls had to be moved to make room for all the building, so the **Mercati di Traiano** (Trajan's Market) was erected on the slopes of Quirinal to accommodate them. The forum and the remains of Trajan's Market, revealing what was formerly a complex system of streets on various levels, with shops, offices and space reserved for public grain distribution, are open to visitors.

The magnificent **Colonna Traiana** (Trajan's Column) towers nearby. Built between AD 107 and 113 to celebrate the victory of Trajan (AD 98–117) over the Dacians, it stands 40 metres (120 ft) high and is covered by a spiral of reliefs depicting Trajan's Dacian campaigns (AD 101–102 and 105). In AD 177, a golden urn containing the remains of the emperor Trajan was buried under the column.

A path leads down to the ruins of the ancient streets that were the political, commercial and religious centre of republican Rome to the **Foro Romano** (Roman Forum). When excavations began in the 18th century, most of this forum was buried under 3 metres (10 ft) of rubble, and the place was known as Campo Vaccino, the cow pasture.

Above: the remains of the Mercati di Traiano

Giolitti

Situated at Via degli Uffici del Vicario 40, this ice-cream parlour serves what are possibly the most delicious ices in the capital – no small claim to fame, considering the Italian passion for ice-cream – and it's well worth making a detour from Via del Corso to get here. Choose from the vast array of mouth-watering flavours available and improve your Italian vocabulary at the same time. *www.giolitti.it*

Lapis Niger (Black Stone)

In front of the Curia lies one of the most sacred objects of Ancient Rome, the Lapis Niger (Black Stone), which is supposed to mark the tomb of Romulus, the mythical founder of the city. The remains of a monument from the 6th century BC have been excavated from under the Lapis Niger and while they do not conclusively prove the existence of the grave, they are evidence that Romulus was already venerated in early Rome.

Museo e Galleria Borghese

The Villa Borghese Museum and Gallery, housed in an early 17th-century *palazzina* designed by the Dutchman, Jan van Santen, is divided into two sections: the sculpture collection, in the museum on the ground floor, and the art collection in the gallery on the first floor. Unfortunately, between 1801 and 1809, the Borghese sculpture collection was severely depleted, when

Above: museum facade, Villa Borghese

more than 200 pieces were sold to the Louvre in Paris. However, there are still some marvellous pieces to be seen. They include some of Bernini's best work, such as *Apollo and Daphne* and *Pluto and Persephone*, as well as Canova's celebrated statue of Pauline Borghese, Napoleon Bonaparte's sister, posing as Venus. The gallery is filled with paintings by the most famous Italian masters of the 16th and 17th centuries: Perugino, Raphael, Botticelli, Caravaggio and Titian. *www.galleriaborghese.it*

Palatino (Palatine Hill)

From the Arch of Titus, the road leads up to Palatino, where the palaces of the Roman emperors once stood. The legend goes that this is where Romulus founded the city, and remains of early 8th-century BC huts have been excavated here. In republican times, the Roman nobility lived on the hill.

Above: *the gardens of Palazzo Farnese, Palatine Hill*

Palazzo Doria Pamphilj

The huge palace on the right at the southern end of Via del Corso is Palazzo Doria Pamphilj, which contains one of the best art collections in Rome, with over 400 paintings from the 15th to the 18th centuries. The gallery walls are plastered with pictures, including a Velázquez portrait of Innocent X and canvasses by Titian, Caravaggio, Lotto and Lorrain.

Palazzo del Quirinale

On one side of Piazza del Quirinale stands Palazzo del Quirinale, which was built as the Pope's summer residence in the 16th century and remained so until 1870, when it became the royal palace of the kings of Italy. Since 1947, it has been the official residence of the President. One section of the palace is open to the public (first and third Sunday of the month). The palace gardens, which stretch far behind the building, are only open to the public once a year, on 2 June, to celebrate the Festa della Repubblica.

Above: inside the vast Pantheon

Pantheon

The Pantheon is the highlight of Rome's Centro Storico (Historic Centre, *see page 32*) and the best-preserved ancient building in the city. It was originally built as a temple to all gods and construction work began in 27 BC, under the orders of the statesman Marcus Agrippa. The temple was turned into a church in AD 609, thus saving the original building from being torn down. The edifice was completely rebuilt by Hadrian (AD 117–138) after a fire. Corinthian columns support a roof with a triangular pediment, and the brick walls are 6 metres (20 ft) thick.

Beneath the porch are 8-metre (24-ft) high bronze doors. Its 45-metre (135-ft) dome, which is 1.6 metres (5 ft) bigger than that of St Peter's, is a perfect hemisphere, a symbol of beauty and harmony. The circular hole *(oculus)* in its centre is still the only source of light.

Originally, the dome was covered in bronze inside and out, but Emperor Constans II is said to have stolen the outer layer to use in Constantinople in 667. Pope Urban VIII of the Barberini family had the inner layer melted down in 1620 in order to make cannons for Castel Sant' Angelo *(see page 30)* and Bernini's *baldacchino* (canopy) in St Peter's *(see page 58–9)*. This act inspired the quip that "what the Barbarians didn't do, the Barberini did."

As with many ancient monuments, the Pantheon

Right: *parade at the Palazzo del Quirinale*

served as a fortress in the Middle Ages, and the notches cut in the portico columns are said to have supported stalls for a fish and poultry market. The marble floor is an 1873 restoration of the original. On opposite sides of the room are the tombs of the first kings of Italy and of the artist Raphael (1483–1520).

Only 15 metres (45 ft) above sea level, the Pantheon is now the lowest point in Rome and it used to flood regularly. The ditch around it shows just how much the rubble has raised Rome over the centuries: in ancient times one looked up to the Pantheon, not down.

Parks in Rome

Rome has many beautiful parks, each with its own attractions. The 17th-century **Doria Pamphilj** *(see also page 40)*, the largest of the city's public parks, has plenty of open spaces and a network of paths, so it is popular with joggers and dog walkers. **Villa**

Above: time for refreshments

Borghese, which is more central than the Doria Pamphilj, is also large and is packed with activities for the kids – you can feed the ducks, hire a rowing boat or bicycle, visit the mini-cinema or zoo and enjoy the small fun fair. Then there are the **Orto Botanico** (Botanical Gardens), behind Palazzo Corsino, which contain more than 7,000 plant species from around the world, including sequoias, palm trees and collections of orchids and bromeliads.

There are also many smaller parks tucked away in little corners, such as the Parco del Celio. They provide some respite, as well as a perfect place for a picnic. Other green spaces include the gardens of Palazzo Farnese, the Pincio Gardens and those of the Villa Celimontana.

Piazza Navona

Piazza Navona stands on the Emperor Domitian's ancient stadium: the stand forms part of the foundations of the flanking houses and you can see one of the original entrances to the north. Its baroque aspect dates from the 17th century, in particular the reign of Innocent X. Some say that the square's name comes from the word *nave*, alluding to its ship-like shape. Others claim it comes from a succession of mutations of *agone*, the word for the Greek-style athletic contests held here: *agone* became *nagone*, which evolved into *navone* and then *navona*.

The stadium was originally 50 by 275 metres (150 by 825 ft), with the seats rising to 35 metres (105 ft). It is thought that it was

Above: statue in the gardens of Villa Borghese

used for athletic contests and horse races and that it was still in use when the Goths invaded in the 5th century. However, the plundering of its fabric began under Constantius II (third son of Constantine the Great), who carried off works of art and decorative features in 356 to adorn his residence in Constantinople.

Nowadays, the square is particularly renowned for its fine fountains, of which two bear the Bernini hallmark: the Fontana dei Quattro Fiumi (Fountain of the Four Rivers), with symbols of the Ganges, the Danube, the Plate and the Nile, and, to the south of the square, the Fontana del Moro (Fountain of the Moor), the central figure of which was designed by Bernini. The Fontana del Nettuno (Fountain of Neptune) was originally just a large basin but the sculptures you see today were added in the 19th century.

Piazza Navona remains today one of the most animated squares in Rome, invariably full of people wandering among stalls set up by hopeful artists or stopping for a coffee in one of the many bars. From December until Epiphany (6 January),

Above: Fontana del Nettuno, Piazza Navona

the square becomes a huge Christmas market, called the Befana after the witch who is believed to bring Italian children either presents or coal, depending on how good they've been.

Piazza del Popolo

Piazza del Popolo, at the northern end of Via del Corso, is one of the most impressive squares in Rome, despite certain questionable connections: the paving was allegedly paid for by taxes levied on prostitutes, and at one time the piazza was used for executions. In the 19th century the square was remodelled by the architect Giuseppe Valadier, who added elegant *pincio* ramps and created the oval form that exists today.

The most striking feature of this elegant square is the obelisk. Stolen from Egypt by the Emperor Augustus, it once decorated the Circus Maximus where it was used as a turning point during chariot races.

Piazza Santa Maria in Trastevere

Via della Scala leads through Piazza Sant' Egidio to Piazza Santa Maria in Trastevere, the heart of the Trastevere neighbourhood. This pedestrianised square is one of the most peaceful in Rome. Many people while away their day in one of the cafes or sitting against Fontana's Fountain (1692), where musicians perform in the summer. The piazza takes its name from the basilica on the east side of the square, one of the oldest in Rome and probably the

Right: *Santa Maria in Trastevere*

first to be dedicated to the Virgin. Its present appearance dates from the 12th century, although the portico (which has recently been cleaned and treated to protect it from the ravages of Rome's pollution) was added in 1702. The 12th- and 13th-century mosaics, both inside and outside the church, are spectacular and it is worth taking a pair of binoculars to enjoy their details. The *Life of the Virgin* series is by Cavallini (1291).

Piazza di Spagna (Spanish Steps)

Piazza di Spagna focuses on the Spanish Steps, so-called because there has been a Spanish Embassy to the Holy See in Palazzo di Spagna since the 17th century. The French owned the land around the convent of Trinità dei Monti at the top of the steps, so claimed the right to pass through the square and named part of it French Square. This petty rivalry between the French and Spanish reached a climax with the building of the Spanish Steps.

Above: the Barcaccia fountain, Piazza di Spagna

The original design of the steps was intended to sing the praises of the French monarchy and there was to have been a huge equestrian statue of Louis XIV displayed here. However, the Pope was against this idea and so when the architect Gaetano de Sanctis finally started construction on the steps in the 18th century, the only reference made to France was the little *fleur-de-lis* that features on the pedestals.

In front of the steps is the fountain by Bernini's father Pietro. *The Barcaccia* is a half-sunken boat fed by water from the ancient aqueduct Acqua Vergine. At the top of the steps is the Trinità dei Monti, which is the city's French church and worth visiting mainly for the the view over the city from its entrance and the damaged *Descent from the Cross* by Da Volterra.

Next to the stairs, in the pink house, is the Keats–Shelley Museum, where the poet John Keats lived in 1820 when he was sent to Rome on account of consumption – Keats's doctor thought that Rome's warm, dry climate would benefit his condition. Keats died the following year, aged just 25.

In 1906, the house was bought by an Anglo-American association and turned into a museum and library dedicated to Keats and fellow Romantics who had made Rome their home for a while. The few rooms open to visitors have personal objects and documents from the lives of Percy Bysshe Shelley and Lord Byron, but the focus is on John Keats – his prints, paintings, books and death mask are on display.

Above: *hanging out at the Spanish Steps*

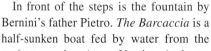

Porta Portese

On Sunday mornings, the big draw in the Trastevere district is the Porta Portese, one of the largest flea markets in Europe, with over 4,000 stalls. When it was established after World War II, the market was a centre for black marketeering. Although its traders are now (for the most part) legal, it is still popular with Romans and visitors alike, and has a great atmosphere.

The market stretches from Porta Portese itself to Viale di Trastevere and reaches nearly as far as Trastevere station. Almost anything you could imagine is on sale here, from the sublime to the ridiculous: antiques, flowers, spare parts for cars, second-hand and new clothes, foodstuffs, comics, china and other household wares. Stallholders flock here from all over Italy and beyond. Some of the more exotic goods for sale include silk shirts from China, all manner of items from Russia, woven fabric and clothes from Latin America, and incense and spices from India. This is probably the most interesting market in Rome,

Above: Piazza di San Giovanni in Laterano

even if the prices – particularly for antiques – have risen sharply in recent years. *www.portaportese.com*

San Clemente

The basilica of San Clemente, in the Lateran district, is one of Rome's best examples of a layered church (where one edifice has been built on top of an older one). Popularly nicknamed "the wedding cake", San Clemente's three layers lie behind an 18th-century facade, behind which is the 12th-century basilica, with a beautifully detailed mosaic depicting the *Triumph of the Cross*. Below this lies the 4th-century church, with fine 11th-century frescoes of miracles being performed by St Clement.

This church is still being excavated by the Dominican monks who live here. The final layer dates from the 1st century, when town houses were converted to a temple dedicated to the god Mithras, for a cult open only to men.

Inside the church, in the Cappella Santa Catterina (St Catherine's Chapel), there are some notable early Renaissance frescoes of the life of St Catherine of Alexandria, painted by Masolino (1383–1447) and Masaccio (1401–28).

San Giovanni in Laterano

On Piazza di San Giovanni, at the heart of the Lateran district, is the mighty basilica of San Giovanni in Laterano – the "mother of all churches" and the first Christian basilica in Rome. Its Apostle figures and the Christ topping

Right: *baptistry, San Giovanni in Laterano*

the facade can be seen as far away as Frascati. Built under Emperor Constantine, the church has stood here since 313 and, although it has burnt down twice and been rebuilt several times, it retains its original structure.

The east facade, through which you enter the church, is the work of Galilei (1732–5), but Fontana designed the north facade when he was working on his rebuilding of the Lateran Palace. Most of the marble-clad interior is the result of remodelling carried out by Borromini (1646), but some of the works of art and church furnishings are far older than this. They include a fragment of

fresco attributed to Giotto (1300) and a 14th-century Gothic *baldacchino* (altar canopy) from which only the Pope is allowed to celebrate Mass (which he does every Maundy Thursday).

The gilded wooden ceiling of the nave, giving it the popular nickname "gilded basilica", was completed in 1567, and had to remain unaltered when Borromini came to work on the building.

Other features of note include the statues of the 12 Apostles designed by followers of Bernini, the baroque frescoes and reliefs of the transept, and the peaceful 13th-century cloisters.

The Battistero Lateranense was part of the original complex here, but it was rebuilt in its present octagonal shape during the 5th century. In the earliest days of

Above: Bernini's masterpiece: Sant' Andrea al Quirinale

Christianity, all Christians were baptised here. The chapels of St John the Evangelist and Santi Rufina e Secunda (the original entrance) contain exquisite 5th-century mosaics.

Sant' Andrea al Quirinale

This, one of the few churches totally designed by Bernini, is located on Via del Quirinale. It creates an awesome impression in spite of its small size. Bernini's theatrical genius is demonstrated by the church's unusual oval plan. Also untypical is the situation of the main facade on the smaller side of the church.

Santa Maria Maggiore

According to legend, in 352 Pope Liberius had a vision of the Virgin Mary, who told him to build a church and to dedicate it to her wherever snow had fallen on the following morning. It was the height of summer, 5 August, but snow was found on the Cispio peak of the Esquiline, and as a result the basilica of Santa Maria Maggiore was built.

The basilica has been rebuilt, extended and embellished since then. The sturdy baroque facade was added during the 18th century. Inside, the coffered ceiling and elaborately decorated chapels are relatively new additions. The ceiling is decorated with some of the first gold brought from the New World. Especially extravagant are the two chapels opposite the altar, dating from the 16th and 17th centuries. The apse mosaic is a 13th-century replacement of the original by Torriti, whereas

Right: the coffered ceiling of Santa Maria Maggiore

the mosaics on the triumphal arch and the panels high up on the nave walls are the original 5th-century ones.

If you happen to be in Rome on 5 August, go to the church to witness white flower petals being showered through a hole in the ceiling in simulation of the miracle.

Stazione Centrale di Termini

One of the few successful pieces of post-war architecture in Rome, the graceful ticket hall of Stazione Termini, as the build-

ing is generally known, alleviates the fascist giantism that otherwise pervades the station. Outside, its forecourt, Piazza dei Cinquecento, is one of the biggest *piazze* in the city (about 400 sq. metres/4,300 sq. ft), yet the square's commanding size does not create a correspondingly big impression, as the piazza is the city's main bus terminus. Food stalls and street vendors add to the general clutter, and the area around the station turns a little seedy when the sun goes down.

During the building of the first station, which opened in 1867, the Mura Serviane (Servian Walls) were uncovered. These are believed to date to the reign of King Tullius Servius in the 6th century BC. During the construction of the present station building, which was completed after World War II, parts of Roman houses and baths were found with their intricate mosaic floors remarkably intact.

Above: Bramante's High-Renaissance tempietto, San Pietro in Montorio

Tempietto di San Pietro in Montorio

When the centre of the Renaissance shifted from northern Italy to Rome at the end of the 15th century, the atmosphere of the Eternal City injected a fresh impetus for the architects of the day to rediscover the styles and motifs of antiquity.

Donato Bramante had learned his trade in the north of Italy and moved to Rome in 1499. The Tempietto di San Pietro in Montorio (1502) was almost the architect's first commission in Rome, but it bears little resemblance to anything he had produced while working in Milan. The Tempietto di San Pietro is the first monument of the High Renaissance style.

Set in an Early Renaissance courtyard, the Tempietto possesses a gravity all of its own. On closer inspection, visitors will see that there is very little surface decoration and that the style of the colonnade – Tuscan Doric – is also unadorned. It supports a classical entablature, which lends further weight and severity

Above: grand facade, Piazza della Repubblica

to the building. These features, combined with the perfect classical proportions, make the Tempietto a quite brilliant homage to antiquity.

Terme di Caracalla (Baths of Caracalla)

When the Terme di Caracalla, on the old Via Appia, were opened in AD 212, they were the largest baths in Rome, with room for 1,600 people. The interior was sumptuously decorated with marble, gilding and coloured stone. Today, only patches of mosaic survive, but the buildings are still impressive, their vaults rising to 30 metres (100 ft).

Bath complexes such as this incorporated other recreational features including gymnasia, libraries and shops; they were also popular places with male and female prostitutes – today, only the females remain. More salubriously, the remains of the *caldarium* (hot room) are used to stage an annual outdoor opera festival in July and August.

Above: *the Terme di Caracalla*

Terme di Diocleziano (Baths of Diocletian)

At the northern end of Piazza dei Cinquecento are the extensive 4th-century remains of the Terme di Diocleziano, which were the largest and most beautiful of the city's 900 bath houses when first built. The *esedra*, the open space surrounded by porticos and seats, is now **Piazza della Repubblica**. The Fontana delle Naiadi (Fountain of the Naiads) set in the centre of the square, dating from *circa* 1900, caused a scandal when it was unveiled, because of the so-called "obscene" postures of the nymphs.

Testaccio

The area to the west of Porta San Paolo is called Testaccio, which was the site of the Port of Rome during Roman times. The name

Testaccio comes from the Latin word testae (meaning "shards"), referring to the many broken pieces of amphorae to be found at the 35 metre- (105 ft-) high Monte Testaccio ("hill of shards"). The amphorae, used to carry imports of oil and wine, were left in this heap once the goods they contained had been unloaded at the port. Today, the hill is all that remains of 400 years of trading oil and wine in Rome.

Porticus Aemelia was constructed in 193 BC, when the old harbour opposite the Bocca della Verità proved to be too small. Trading ships would have docked in Piazza dell'Emporio and the amphorae would then have been unloaded. The harbour warehouses must have been massive, as it is known that 294

Right: Fontana delle Naiadi, Piazza della Repubblica

pillars supported the roof alone. Important remains can be seen in Via Branca, Via Rubattino and Via Florio, as well as on the banks of the Tiber in front of Lungotevere Testaccio.

Università Romana (University of Rome)

The venerable Università Romana was founded in 1303 by Pope Boniface VIII. From the reign of Pope Eugene IV (1431–47) until 1935, it was based in Palazzo della Sapienza, in the heart of the city, but in 1935, when the Città Universitaria was inaugurated, it moved to its present site in the San Lorenzo Quarter. The new campus was designed in the modern classical style favoured by fascist leaders – big, white and imposing – by Marcello Piacentini from 1933 to 1935, in accordance with a plan that involved two axes intersecting at a right angle in the Piazzale del Rettorato.

However, the equilibrium was upset following World War II, when more buildings were added to the complex to house the grow-

ing number of students. The interior has been as well planned as the exterior, with modern paintings on the walls. The library, Biblioteca Universitaria Alessandrina, houses one million books and 16,000 journals.

The San Lorenzo area is known as the student quarter and its streets are packed with bars and inexpensive *trattorie* and *pizzerie*.

Above: the Basilica di San Pietro (St Peter's), from Piazza San Pietro

Vaticano (Vatican)

The fabulous extravagance of the Catholic Church through the ages is celebrated without restraint in the Vatican State. The Basilica di San Pietro (St Peter's Church, *see page 58*) alone is impressive, with its huge dimensions, vast dome designed by Michelangelo and an interior sumptuously bedecked with Bernini's glistening creations. Then there are the Musei Vaticani (Vatican Museums, *see page 61*) – mile upon mile of rooms and corridors containing historic treasures, the world-famous Cappella della Sistina (Sistine Chapel, *see page 59*) and the Raphael Rooms *(see page 61)*.

The Vatican, with the Pope as supreme ruler, is the world's smallest independent state, with a population of approximately 500 people, of which only around 300 actually live there. Founded in 1929, the papal state has its own stamps, currency, media, railway and police force (the Swiss Guards, *see page 61*).

In ancient times, Nero's Circus occupied the site where the Vatican now stands, and St Peter, apparently, was crucified upside-down here and buried close by. The early Christians built a modest little chapel to commemorate the saint and a couple of hundred years later Constantine built his huge basilica here. *www.vatican.va*

Right: *crowds gather to hear the Pope's blessing on Easter Sunday*

BASILICA DI SAN PIETRO

St Peter's is an architectural mishmash. The original Constantinian church was of the typical basilican form – a Latin-cross with a nave, side aisles and a crossing. However, in 1452, Nicholas V, deciding that the church was in need of restoration and enlargement, initiated a programme of building. In 1506, Bramante, under Julius II, started work on a new centrally planned Greek-cross church, but after his death, Raphael, da Sangallo and Fra Giacondo took over, and reverted to a Latin-cross church. In 1546, Michelangelo opted once again for the Greek-cross and designed the dome.

After Michelangelo's death in 1564, the architects Della Porta and Fontana continued his work until Pope Paul V decided that the Latin-cross was more appropriate. Another architect, Maderno, added the parts necessary for the change and completed the facade. In 1629, Bernini constructed the twin towers framing the facade designed by Maderno, but they were torn down when one tower was found to be causing the Basilica to crumble.

Above: elaborate architecture at the Vatican

One of the main attractions inside St Peter's, just to the right of the entrance, is *La Pietà*, Michelangelo's glorious rendering of the Madonna and dead Christ, which he sculpted when only 25. Other highlights include three works by Bernini: a statue of Constantine on a galloping horse (on the left as you pass into the portico), his *baldacchino*, a huge bronze canopy right under the dome and over the legendary tomb of St Peter and, on the apse wall, framed by the *baldacchino*, the "Cattedra Petra", a gilded wooden chair that was reputedly used by Peter when preaching his first sermon. On the right-hand side of the portico is the entrance to Michelangelo's dome. The long climb to the top is rewarded by extensive views across the city.

PIAZZA SAN PIETRO

The great square in front of St Peter's Basilica was created by Bernini between 1656 and 1667 for Alexander VII. Its two semicircular wings represent the outstretched arms of the church, embracing and protecting the congregation. In the centre are fountains by Maderno and Della Fontana, and an Egyptian obelisk, originally from Heliopolis, placed here by Sixtus V.

CAPELLA SISTINA (SISTINE CHAPEL)

No visit to the Vatican is complete without a trip inside the Sistine Chapel. To see it, you need to enter the Musei Vaticani (Vatican Museums; *see page 61*). Be warned: the museums are large

Right: the Swiss Guards, the papal police corps

and the Sistine Chapel is about 20 minutes' walk from the entrance. It's worth the walk, however, since the chapel walls depicting scenes from the lives of Christ and Moses are painted by some of the greatest masters of the Italian Renaissance: Botticelli, Perugino, Ghirlandaio and Signorelli. And that's without mentioning the ceiling…

To paint his Old Testament masterpiece, Michelangelo worked single-handedly – and upside-down – for four years. The ceiling depicts scenes from the book of Genesis, starting with God dividing light from dark and ending with the drunkenness of Noah, seen in reverse from the entrance. The sides show the ancestors of Christ (in the triangles) and, on marble thrones, the prophets and the classical *sybils* who prophesised Christ's coming.

Above these are the *ignudi*, nude figures holding up festoons with papal symbols and medallions. In the four corners are scenes of salvation, including the dramatic hanging of Haman and Judith swiping off Holofernes's head.

Above: *"Fire in the Borgo", Raphael Rooms, Musei Vaticani*

The ceiling has no fixed point of view, no single system of perspective and no one clear meaning. Critics cannot agree if the ceiling is a neo-Platonic statement or a theological programme devised with the help of religious experts, including perhaps Julius II.

Some critics say the general theme is salvation, reaching its climax in the *Last Judgment* fresco on the end wall (painted by Michelangelo between 1535 and 1541 and restored in 1994). It depicts a harrowing image of the souls of the dead rising up to face the wrath of God. The good are promoted to heaven, while the damned are cast down into hell.

MUSEI VATICANI (VATICAN MUSEUMS)

Passing round the monumental walls designed by Michelangelo, you reach the entrance to the Vatican Museums. Leading up to the ticket offices is the entertaining spiral ramp (1932), which will make your head spin if you try to work it out. On entering the museums, decide what you want to see and then follow the colour-coded route taking in the items on your list. The routes vary in length from 90 minutes to five hours. Highlights include the Sistine Chapel *(see above)* and the Raphael Rooms, housing numerous masterpieces by the great painter.

SWISS GUARDS

Founded in 1506 by Pope Julius II, the first members of the Swiss Guards were recruited from Switzerland, hence their name. They were enlisted from the mercenaries of the cantons of the Swiss

Above: Swiss Guard on ceremony

confederacy because they had established a reputation for themselves as excellent infantrymen following their victory over the Burgundian cavalry in 1476.

Their role nowadays, however, as papal police corps, is mainly ceremonial. They wear a distinctive and picturesque dark blue, yellow and red uniform – the colours of the Medici popes – consisting of pantaloons gathered below the knee and a full-sleeved jacket, which is alleged to have been designed for them by Michelangelo. They are armed with a halberd (a tall spear that includes an axe blade and a pick) and a sword.

Via Appia (Appian Way)

In classical times, Via Appia, named after Appius Claudius Caecus under whose magistracy the road opened in 312 BC, began at the Circus Maximus and passed the Baths of Caracalla on its way to the city gate of Porta Appia (now Porta San Sebas-

Above: the Circo di Massenzio (Circus of Maxentius), Via Appia

tiano) in the Aurelian Walls. Today, only the section of the road outside the ancient Porta Appia is called Via Appia. The stretch leading up to the Porta San Sebastiano is called Via di Porta San Sebastiano.

Via Condotti

Halfway along Via del Corso *(see below)* is Via Condotti, designer-label heaven *(see page 21)*. This street, plus the parallel streets of Via Borgognona and Via Frattina, which are linked by the equally sumptuous Via Bocca di Leone, are home to all the top fashion outlets. Matching the expensive shops are some of the best hotels in Rome.

Via del Corso

Via del Corso links Piazza del Popolo (for centuries the main entrance to Rome for travellers coming from the north) with Piazza Venezia, long one of Rome's central squares. The name "Corso" dates from the 15th century when Pope Paul II introduced horse racing *(corsi)* along its length. Pope Alexander VII had the road straightened in the 16th century.

The races were imitations of the ancient games (with all their atrocities) and it wasn't only horses that ran: there were races for prostitutes, children, Jews and cripples. The races were finally banned at the end of the 19th century.

Right: shopping in the Via Condotti area

These days, the only people racing along the Corso are politicians being whisked at high speed to Palazzo Chigi in Piazza Colonna, the prime minister's official residence, and the neighbouring Palazzo Montecitorio, the meeting place for the chamber of Deputies, the Italian Parliment.

Piazza Colonna marks a divide in the street: the stretch from here to Piazza Venezia is lined with huge palaces, mainly homes to banks, whereas the stretch to Piazza del Popolo is a partly pedestrianised area where shoppers browse windows displaying *svago* (leisure) and fashion wear. In the early evening and on Saturdays, this is a popular spot with Romans taking a stroll.

Via Giulia

The road to the left of Palazzo Farnese leads to Via Giulia, named after Pope Julius II, who commissioned it as a monument to the Apostolic Church. When Bramante began work on the road

Above: *taking a break in Piazza Farnese*

in 1508, he meant to make it Rome's most important thoroughfare, connecting the Vatican with Ponte Sisto and the Ripa Grande harbour, and thus the centre of Papal Rome. The centrepiece of the street was to be the Tribunal Palace. Bramante started work on this but building failed to get beyond the foundations stage – these can still be seen between Vicolo del Cefalo and Via del Gonfalone.

In later years, the street became a chic address and many famous people lived in its fine palaces, including the painters Raphael and Benvenuto Cellini. The parties in Via Giulia were among the best in Rome and on one occasion wine is said to have gushed from the nearby Mascherone Fountain for three full days. All this is hard to believe now, as the street is quiet, in parts traffic-free, and lined with up-market antiques shops and art galleries.

The elegant arch across the street was designed by Michelangelo and was intended to connect Palazzo Farnese with Villa Farnesina across the Tiber. The bridge, however, was never built.

Vittoriano

The white edifice in front of Palazzo Doria Pamphilj is the Vittoriano (built from 1885), a monument to Vittorio Emanuele II and the site of the tomb of the unknown soldier. Dubbed an "enormous white cancerous tumour" by the poet Gabriele d'Annunzio, the building is often called the "typewriter", owing to its design.

Right: elegant facades on Piazza Farnese

ESSENTIAL INFORMATION

The Place

Ancient Rome was built on and between seven hills: the Capitoline, Palatine, Viminale, Esquiline, Celio, Aventine and Quirinale, and these still occupy the centre, although they are now barely discernible as distinct hills. The modern inner city, which is classified as being inside the Aurelian Wall and is divided into *rioni*, covers around 21 sq. km (8 sq. miles). The outer city covers an area of around 150 sq. km (58 sq. miles), while the province of Rome, which includes among others the Castelli Romani, covers 5,352 sq. km (2,066 sq. miles). The Vatican state covers an area of about 0.4 hectares (1 acre); it has an official population of 500 people but only around 300 actually live there.

Population: central Rome: 3 million

Language: Italian

Time zone: Central European Time (GMT + 1 hour)

Currency: Italian Lire

Weights and measures: metric

Electricity: 220 volts. Two-pin plugs.

International dialling code: 39 for Italy, 06 for Rome

The Climate

The city has a mild Mediterranean climate, the coldest month being January, with a mean temperature of 8°C (46°F). In April the average temperature is around 14°C (57°F), while in August the mean temperature is about 25°C (77°F), although there are days when it is as hot as 40°C (104°F). On average, the sun shines for more than 180 days a year; the wettest month is October.

Left: the lavish Borge Santo Spirito

The Economy

The city has a predominantly service economy with around 600,000 office workers compared to an industrial workforce of only 100,000. The civil service is the biggest employer. Nearly all sections of society contrive to avoid paying money to the Government, as a result of which the underground economy, the *economia sommersa*, is very powerful.

Public Holidays

Banks and most shops close on the following public holidays:
New Year's Day *(Capodanno)*: 1 January
Epiphany *(Befana)*: 6 January
Easter Monday *(Lunedí di Pasqua)*: variable
Liberation Day *(Anniversario della Liberazione)*: 25 April
May Day *(Festa del Lavoro)*: 1 May
Patron Saints of Rome Day *(Santi Pietro e Paolo)*: 29 June
August holiday *(Ferragosto)*: 15 August

Above: book-hunting at the flea market, Porta Portese

All Saints Day (*Ognissanti*): 1 November
Immaculate Conception (*Immacolata Concezione*): 8 December
Christmas Day (*Natale*): 25 December
Boxing Day (*Santo Stefano*): 26 December

Getting There

BY AIR

There are direct scheduled flights to Rome from most major European cities, Australia and a number of cities in North America. From many European countries, there are also charter flights.

Scheduled flights land at the main airport, Aeroporto Leonardo da Vinci in Fiumicino, around 30 km (18 miles) southwest of Rome. There is a frequent train service to the city from here. Charters come into Ciampino airport, about 15 km (9 miles) southeast of the city. The best way to reach the centre of Rome from here is by taxi.

BY RAIL

Rome is well served by rail links to most major European cities, and the national railway, Ferrovia dello Stato, is generally efficient and fairly inexpensive (note that supplements are usually payable on the fast Eurostar, EuroCity, Inter City and Pendolino services). Stazione Termini is Rome's main railway station, the meeting point of the two metro lines and the main bus stop for many city buses.

Train tickets are valid for two

Right: *ready for the next fare*

months after the date of issue and must be stamped on the day you travel at one of the machines at the stations. For train enquiries across Italy, tel: 147-888088.

BY ROAD

European Union driving licences are valid in Italy. Travellers from other countries normally require an international driving licence. You must have your licence plus the vehicle registration and insurance (Green Card) documents with you when driving.

The A1 Autostrada del Sole (toll payable) leads into the Gran Raccordo Anulare (GRA), the busy ring motorway around Rome, from north and south, as does the A24 from the east. If you arrive on the Via del Mare from the coast (Ostia), you can switch onto

the GRA or continue straight on into the centre.

When leaving the GRA, follow the white signs for the road you want (most blue signs lead away from the centre). Look for the centre sign: a black point in a black circle on a white background.

If you are travelling to Rome by coach, you will probably arrive either at or near to Stazione Termini.

Visas and passports

European Union passport holders do not require a visa – a valid passport is sufficient. Visitors from the US, Canada, Australia or New Zealand do not require visas for stays of up to three months.

Above: reading in the sun

Nationals from the majority of other countries will need a visa. This must be obtained in advance from the Italian Consulate.

Health

In summer, heat and sunshine may pose problems for those not used to Mediterranean climates. Although some Roman hotels and restaurants now have air conditioning, many more do not. This means you will probably need to keep the windows open, and inevitably risk introducing mosquitos. Make sure you bring mosquito repellent with you.

Tap water in Rome is generally perfectly drinkable, especially from street fountains – the water comes from the same natural springs used by the ancient Romans. Exceptions are marked *acqua non potabile*. In the event of an emergency, the telephone number for an ambulance is **113**.

Disabled Travellers

Rome does not, in general, cater well for the disabled. With the exception of the Musei Vaticani, most public buildings have little or no disabled access. Streets and pavements are often uneven, and many pavements in the medieval centre are too narrow and uneven for a wheelchair. Some trains have access for the disabled, but check (tel: 147-888088) before travelling. Although

Above: *asking for directions*

seats at the front of city buses are reserved for the disabled, buses and trams may be difficult to use. If travelling by car, you can make use of free parking spaces for disabled drivers if you have an official placard.

A number of Roman hotels now claim to offer access to disabled travellers but it's always best to call and check in advance, being as precise as possible about your needs. The same goes for restaurants.

Currency

The decision to replace the lira (plural lire) as Italy's main unit of currency with the euro from January 2002 meant the end of bills that sometimes looked like telephone numbers. Major credit cards are accepted by the majority of hotels, shops and restaurants. Automated cash dispensers *(Bancomat)* can be found throughout central Rome; these are linked with several international banking systems, including Visa and Cirrus.

Note, however, that very few petrol stations accept credit cards or travellers' cheques. Travellers' cheques are accepted in most banks, although changing them can be a lengthy process.

Banks are open Monday–Friday 8.30am–1.30pm and 2.45–3.45pm. Note that you will need to produce your passport or identification card when changing money in a bank.

Above: keeping law and order on the streets

Security and Crime

The main problem for tourists in Rome is petty crime: pick-pocketing, bag snatching and theft from parked cars. Take particular care if you are near Stazione Termini, as the area around this station is known for drug peddling and prostitution.

Reduce the possibility of theft by taking some elementary precautions. Leave money and valuables, including airline tickets, in the hotel safe. Carry your camera out of sight and always be discreet with your money or wallet.

One Roman speciality is the motorbike snatch, so if you are carrying a handbag, keep it on the side away from the road; if you are sitting in a cafe, place your handbag firmly on your lap. Backpacks, while convenient, make easy targets for pickpockets, so take them off or sling them under your arm, especially if you are in a crowd.

Where to Stay

Rome offers countless places to stay in every imaginable category. The area around Piazza Navona, the Pantheon and Campo de' Fiori perhaps offers the best introduction to the city, since here you are right in its medieval heart and within easy reach of almost all the main sights. However, there are relatively few hotels in the area, and these tend to book up early. This area is always lively, which does mean that it is noisy.

Right: Hotel Cesari, off Via del Corso

For a quieter, although less central, location, try the Aventine Hill. The Via Veneto area is much handier for the city centre but the hotels here are mostly at the higher end of the scale; there is a more varied selection around Piazza di Spagna. Large numbers of hotels can be found around Stazione Termini, although this is not the most attractive area and the area just to the south of the station is best avoided.

The Rome Tourist Office (EPT) publishes an annual list *(Annuario Alberghi)* showing star categories, facilities and prices of all Rome hotels, obtainable from the Rome EPT direct or through Italian national tourist offices. Commission-free booking is available from the Hotel Reservation Service in Stazione Termini.

While hotels in Rome are rated by stars, these ratings correspond to facilities and services offered, and not to the quality, which is often disappointing compared with what you would expect from similarly rated hotels in other major European cities.

Bed and breakfasts in the city offer an economical alternative

to hotels. Note, however, that they vary considerably in terms of quality, although they must meet minimum standards of cleanliness and amenities. Many are nothing more than a private room in someone's home. The EPT office on Via Parigi 5 has a full listing of registered bed and breakfasts.

Above: *service with a smile*

Useful Addresses

TOURIST OFFICES IN ROME

Main Rome Tourist Office (EPT): Via Parigi 5. Tel: 06-4889 9253/5.

Also at: Largo Goldoni; Castel Sant'Angelo; Via dei Fori Imperiali; Piazza Cinque Lune; Via Nazionale; Piazza Sonnino (Trastevere); Piazza San Giovanni; Santa Maria Maggiore; Stazione Termini.

TOURIST OFFICES OUTSIDE ITALY

UK: Italian State Tourist Office, 1 Princes Street, London W1. Tel: 020-7408 1254.
US: Italian Government Tourist Office, 630 5th Avenue, Suite 1565, New York, NY 10111. Tel: 212 245 4822/3/4.

CONSULATE ADDRESSES

UK: Via XX Settembre 80/A. Tel: 06-4825441.
US: Via Veneto 121. Tel: 06-46741.

Useful Websites

- *www.inroma.it* (general information)
- *www.enjoyrome.com* (general listings)
- *www.christusrex.org/www1/vaticano* (extensive Vatican/Sistine Chapel information)
- *www.inroma.it/cultura/musei/index* (Roman museums)
- *www.informaroma.it* (Official City of Rome database)
- *www.comune.roma.it* (Official City of Rome site)

Right: angel by Bernini

The Vatican

VATICAN TOURIST OFFICE

Ufficio Informazioni, Pellegrini e Turisti, Braccio Carlo Magno, Piazza San Pietro (to the left of the church).

PAPAL AUDIENCES

To attend an audience with the Pope, you should write to the Prefettura della Casa Pontificia, Città del Vaticano 00120 (tel: 06-69883273). Specify the date you wish to attend and give a local phone number and address (your hotel). The general audiences are held in St Peter's Square or in the Audience room or, in summer, at Castel Gandolfo, the Pope's summer residence in the Castelli Romani. There is no charge for attending an audience.

Activities for Children

Rome is not an obvious place to choose for a children's holiday, but Italian culture is very hospitable towards children. After-

noon *siestas* may help your offspring – and yourself – cope with the heat at midday.

Food should not pose too many problems, as the majority of children enjoy pasta and pizza, and these are both readily available – in many forms. Restaurants do not usually open until 8pm, so if you have small children who need to eat earlier than that, look for a bar

Above: coffee and a chat

or *rosticceria* serving snacks and meals. If you are travelling with a baby, note that changing facilities in Rome are scarce and difficult to find.

Children are likely to enjoy visits to the Via Appia, the catacombs and the Museum of the Walls, the Colosseum and major Roman ruins in the Forum and Terme di Caracalla (Baths of Caracalla), St Peter's and its dome, and the Castel Sant'Angelo. Puppet theatre is also worth looking out for.

If children need relief from Rome's busy streets, there are a number of green spaces within easy reach of the centre such as Villa Borghese and Doria Pamphilj.

Gay Rome

Rome has an active and vibrant gay community. The national magazine, *Babilonia*, is published monthly and should be available from most newsstands. There is a national gay festival in May. For further information on the gay scene, contact: ARCI GAY, tel: 06-4465836.

Above: testing the "Mouth of Truth" at Santa Maria in Cosmedin

Basic Italian

Yes *Sì*
No *No*
Please *Per favore*
Thank you *Grazie*
Hello/Hi/Bye *Ciao*
Hello (Good day) *Buon giorno*
Good evening *Buona sera*
Goodbye *Arrivederci*
Do you speak English? *Parla inglese?*
I don't understand *Non capisco*
Could you speak more slowly? *Può parlare piu lentamente?*
When/Why/Where? *Quando/Perchè/Dove?*

What *Quale/Come...?*
yesterday/today/tomorrow *ieri/oggi/domani*
Do you have any vacant rooms? *Avete camere libere?*
Have you got a table for... *Avete un tavolo per ...*
I have a reservation *Ho fatto una prenotazione*
I'd like... *Vorrei...*
How much is it? *Quanto costa?*
Where is the lavatory? *Dov'è il bagno?*
Can I have the bill, please? *Posso avere il conto, per favore.*

Above: the Fontana di Trevi

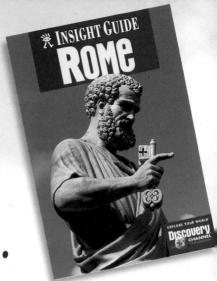

Also from Insight Guides...

Insight Guides is the award-winning classic series that provides the complete picture of a destination, with expert and informative text and the world's best photography. Each book has everything you need, being an ideal travel planner, a reliable on-the-spot guide, and a superb souvenir of a trip. Nearly 200 titles.

Insight Maps are designed to complement the guidebooks. They provide full, clear mapping of major destinations, list top sights, and their laminated finish makes them durable and easy to fold. More than 100 titles.

Insight Compact Guides are handy reference books, modestly priced but comprehensive. Text, pictures and maps are all cross-referenced, making them ideal books for on-the-spot use. 120 titles.

Insight Pocket Guides pioneered the concept of the authors as "local hosts" who provide personal recommendations, just as they would give honest advice to a friend. Pull-out map included. 120 titles.

☆ INSIGHT GUIDES

The world's largest collection of visual travel guides